Leanne is a poet, performer ar
Norfolk. An award-winning writer,
fledgling theatre-maker, Leanne
the Edinburgh Fringe, Sofar Sou
Cambridge and TEDx WOMEN at UCL in London. —
the Paper Crane Poets collective in Beeston, and is a founding
member of 28 Sonnets Later. Leanne's work has appeared in
publications and gallery spaces in the UK, USA, Spain, Iraq and
Israel, and she once stood next to someone famous in a pub in
Suffolk. She lives in Nottingham with her partner and their cat,
Brambles.

www.leannemoden.com

Cover illustration by Hannah Radenkova
www.hannahradenkova.co.uk

GET OVER YOURSELF

LEANNE MODEN

Burning Eye

BurningEyeBooks
Never Knowingly
Mainstream

Supported using public funding by
**ARTS COUNCIL
ENGLAND**
LOTTERY FUNDED

This edition published by Burning Eye Books 2020

www.burningeye.co.uk

@burningeyebooks

Burning Eye Books
15 West Hill, Portishead, BS20 6LG

ISBN 978-1-911570-87-5

GET OVER YOURSELF

CONTENTS

NIGHTCLIMBING

Take my hand
and we'll rise above all this.
Because you need a fresh perspective
and somewhere near here, there's a hole in the fence
with both our names on it.

If you need me to, I will lace my fingers together
to build your first step up.
So come on! Feel the footholds worn into the walls and
grip the crumbling brickwork with both hands.

Kiss every grotesque as you climb, but don't look down –
instead, heave your body skyward and watch the stars come
out.

Soon we'll be standing on the shoulders of kings,
the wind at our backs as the city tumbles away from us.
An anarchy of rooftops
waiting to be conquered.

Spires stooped against shopping centres and office blocks.
Each building burst from the ground like a mushroom,
luminous with ambition, forcing its way into being.

You see, this town grew up from the dirt,
its foundations unstable.
And everyone said that it wouldn't last.
But look at us now.

We made it this far
but we're not in it for the glory.

We just needed a new perspective.

And, while we may not have the keys to this city,
we know how to scale the walls.

Let's climb every college, leap across the parapets
and claim these rooftops for anyone who has ever
been excluded

because this city is ours tonight
and we can do anything.

POISON

after David Allan Evans

Every time I smell that perfume it is 1996.
My mother is seated at the scuffed wooden
table in our yellow-walled kitchen, her striped
Gateway uniform pulled up around her collar
where she sprays the perfume, just a little,
onto the skin behind her ears. Then she goes out
into the dark to stack tins and cut ready meals free
from plastic pallets. The tins and ready meals that
pass into the hands of early morning shoppers, who
have no clue how they got there. But my mother is
not tins and ready meals and box-cutters and the
stripes of the Gateway uniform. She is the yellow-
walled kitchen, and the scuffed kitchen table, and
the hint of Dior clinging to the skin behind her ears.

RECOVERING

instead of a heart monitor
there is the beat of drums
instead of an artificial lung
there is a bass keeping time
instead of an intravenous line
there is a headphone wire
instead of nerves on fire
there is a microphone
instead of blood and bone
there are brutal melodies
this is not radio therapy
this is a wall of sound
as skull hits glass hits ground
with lyrics speaking truthfully
making sense of what you see
so take this as a sign
it may not be okay for a long time
wounds like these take years to heal
and you can't change the way you feel
but skipped-track arrhythmia
and scratched-CD-surface scars
tell us who we really are
so tell us who you really are

SMALL TOWN BLUES (WISBECH, 2002)

If you love empty fields and a well-constructed ditch
then this town is the place to scratch your panoramic itch.
It's featureless and flat here, but that's not the only hitch;
our businesses are failing, but our soil is really rich.

Despite the name, we have no beach – and very little whizz;
we frequently score high on poverty analysis.
And you may call it bleak, but then the point you're missing is
that once a month the Black Bear does a really good pub quiz.

We haven't got a bookshop, but our bingo hall's a winner
and you can smoke in Terry's while you're trying to eat your dinner.
There's something almost charming in the greyness of the river
and the fair that comes to town just when the weather's turning
    bitter.

Old ladies in the cafés laughing hoarsely like hyenas,
the smell of frying burgers in the vans at the arena,
the subtle whiff of cat food being canned down at Purina:
all these things contribute to the town's unique demeanour.

Our chief exports are vegetables and rampant xenophobia,
declining manufacturing and civic-led myopia.
We've only got one Catholic church, and so we could be pope-ier,
and every year more shops close down; the high street's getting
    ropier.

Our football team is non-league and tenaciously subpar.
We haven't got a nightclub or a single decent bar.
The nearest town is fifteen miles and, if you've got no car,
that's fifty minutes on the bus to your local cinema.

We've got a castle, three museums and a brewery,
but precious little in the way of opportunity.
We haven't had an A&E since 1983
and there's nowhere in town to do your A-levels for free.

The comprehensive's failing and the grammar costs a bomb,
the queue outside the job centre is getting pretty long,
the smell of onions being picked is really fucking strong,
and everyone just lives their lives as if there's nothing wrong.

It's like the 1940s came and never went away:
a town that's lost in time, but in a disappointing way.
So, just like every pop-punk song or teenage film cliché,
I'm waiting for my life to start, so I can get away.

SIX MONTHS ABROAD

Half a story,
half a lie,
half a moon
in half a sky.

Half a ticket,
booked in haste.
Half the roti,
half the taste.

Half a mattress,
half a chair.
Half expecting,
half aware.

Henna gracing
half a hand.
Half prepared and
half unplanned.

Half an adult,
half a child;
half content,
half running wild.

Half a ship
with sail unfurled,
half the way
across the world.

Half a yawn
and half a sigh.
Half the pill means
half the high.

Half in awe
and half afraid
that half will go
while half might stay.

Half enlightened,
half naïve.
Half-lived truths
still half believed.

Most ambitions
half achieved.
Half confused
and half relieved.

EVERYTHING'S FINE

This is the 'Everything's Fine' alarm,
which we've installed so that you know

Everything's Fine.

It takes a bit of getting used to,
but the ringing in your ears will fade
after four to six weeks
and cases of alarm-induced tinnitus
have not been scientifically proven.

Are you sure you didn't have it before you came here?

Don't worry if you can't remember, because

Everything's Fine.

Relax.

Everything's Fine.

Don't worry if you have to
raise your voice; conversation is
overrated anyway. Especially now, because

Everything's Fine.

Relax; we've done extensive laboratory testing
to confirm that

Everything's Fine.

All the surveys we've conducted
came back with the same result:

Everything's Fine.

You might experience some temporal
cognitive impairment, but that's normal,
and, anyway, that doesn't even matter that much
now that

Everything's Fine.

Relax. There's nothing left to worry about.
You may not be able to catch every word,
or even be able to hear yourself think,
but thinking is overrated anyway.

And the only thing you need to think about now
is the fact that

                                        Everything's Fine.

Only five percent of people
experience the dizziness,
and that nausea you're feeling
will settle soon, because, as you can hear,

                                        Everything's Fine.

And, really, isn't the odd migraine
a small price to pay to ensure that

                                        Everything's Fine?

Should you experience any bleeding
from your ears, you can be safe in the knowledge that
actually

                                        Everything's Fine.

Don't worry about any noises
you might hear outside,
the ones that sound like explosions,
and rioting, and hordes of hostile undead
tearing at the perimeter fencing.

WE'LL JUST TURN UP THE ALARM

because

                                        Everything's Fine.

There's nothing left to worry about.

Stay calm. Don't panic.

                                        Everything's Fine.

There's no need to be afraid;
as long as you can hear the alarm,

                              Everything's Fine.

The smell of smoke is normal,
the heat on your face is normal,
the sound of the siren is normal.

Don't worry. As long as the alarm is on

                              Everything's Fine.

19

ON BECOMING

Today, I am black lipstick.
Wilful, disobedient.
I am oil-slick grin,
thick black outline.
I am bird's wing;
I am beast's flank.
I am opaque and I am limitless.

Today, I am black lipstick.
Headstrong, intractable.
I am burning meteorite,
collapsing supernova.
I am wet mouth;
I am echoing ventricle.
I am magnetic and I am outrageous.

Today, I am black lipstick.
Deliberate, considered.
I am ocean floor
and space between stars.
I am lip-taste;
I am skin-shine.
I am equilibrium and I am disparity.

Today, I am black lipstick.
Transgressive, unflinching.
I am incautious uncertainty,
trepidation but not fear.
I am experimentation;
I am complication.
I am confidence and I am indecision.

I am not beautiful, but I am powerful.
I am powerful and that is beautiful.

Today, I am black lipstick,
and that is enough.

BAD KISSER

When we first met, I found you quite charming,
but that impression began to cave in
the first time that I let you kiss me
and you licked me from forehead to chin.

I knew that you weren't great with women;
now I finally understood why –
being able to suck on my tonsils
is not something I want in a guy.

I still feel the pang of revulsion
when I think of your molars on mine.
The clash of enamel connecting
sending chills to the base of my spine.

I know you were just keen to please me,
but your performance was really bizarre.
You formed a tight seal round my head holes –
it's not meant to be like CPR.

I'm going to give you some feedback:
please know that I'm not one to quibble,
but we women don't like to be moistened
with silvery ribbons of dribble.

Not that it wasn't impressive,
the incredible girth of your tongue,
but the ravenous way that you wield it!
You damn nearly punctured my lung!

But, now that you're gone, I feel lonely.
Normal kisses just don't fill the space.
Turns out that, although I protested,
I still want you to suck on my face.

You were gnawing the tonsils of some girl
in the precinct by Iceland today,
and I know for a fact that I've lost you.
The bad kisser who slipped clean away.

GUIDELINES

Come out tonight.
Come at midnight and come with us.
Don't worry about what you're wearing
as long as what you're wearing is black.
Come for warm bodies and sweat, spit and cigarettes,
whiskey and mixers, lipstick and fishnets.
Tear your tights on someone else's fingernails,
shout secrets into the speakers and throw your fists in the air.
Move and twist and strut.
Don't worry about how you're dancing
as long as you are dancing –
the beat is only a guideline anyway.

Come out tonight.
Come prepared and come with us.
Don't worry about what you're drinking
as long as we're drinking too.
Come for best mates and heartbreak, vomit and glory,
music and mayhem, connection, tall stories.
Wear your heart like a brand-new T-shirt:
don't let anyone get shit on it!
Shout and screech and scream.
Don't worry about what you're singing
as long as you are singing –
the words are only a guideline anyway.

Come out tonight.
Come late and come with us.
Don't worry about what they call you
as long as they call you something.
Come for black nails and tattoos, dyed hair and scuffed shoes;
come and be whoever you choose to be.
Share songs with girls you've been too scared to speak to
and scream your frustrations into someone else's shoulder
blades.

Laugh and cry and rage.
Don't worry about how you're feeling
as long as you are feeling –
your emotions are only a guideline anyway.

Remember, you are not here to impress the boys in the band,
so get dancing.
You are not here to sit in the corner on your own,
so get dancing.
You are not here unless you're at the front,
so get dancing.

This gig is for you
and for everyone who felt like they didn't matter:
you matter.

So get dancing.
The beat is only a guideline anyway.

TUESDAY EVENING, TEN FORTY-SIX

This evening, we are buying vodka.
Just for something to do.

Our corner shop is
twenty minutes from town,
but we always make the pilgrimage
because here, we are kings!

Here, normal rules do not apply
and we are untouchable.
The owner doesn't care how old we are
as long as we have ten pounds
between us, and we don't make
too much noise.

We are quiet kings here,
and kings deserve vodka.

But all is not well in this kingdom tonight.

There are three of them,
blond hair, uneven teeth,
girls we've seen too many times before
following us
like they're planning a coup.

We shrug off their glances like threadbare robes,
make jokes and take things off shelves
to show one another
we are invincible, here. Untouchable.
Experts in ignoring unwanted attention.

We are kings;
we are here to buy vodka;
we are not looking for trouble.

Our kingdom is grey floor tiles,
handwritten price tags on starbursts of
cardboard. Rows of toothpaste
stand like sentinels
as the first fist connects.

We have no armies to defend us
even in our own lands. And in real life
battles are not choreographed,
so the grasping grappling desperation
takes us all by surprise. The shouting, the spit,
the smell of body spray masking sweat.

We are all translucent now
like cheap vodka
and the shopkeeper,
reflected in the curved security mirror,
widens his eyes in warning.

A blade withdrawn from a scabbard
or a rucksack or the pocket of a tracksuit.
A stack of cans tumbling to the floor.

I kick, make contact with a shin.
One girl stumbles into another.
They let go of your coat and we run.

We run.

We run and we don't stop
until we reach the floodlit bus station.

There is blood at my temple.
A scratch,
but enough to unsettle us.

We cover it with jokes and dismissals,
but our crowns have slipped,
our sceptres dented.

We roll thin filterless cigarettes,
smoke them, roll more,
ask whether the pub
will serve us this late,

and I grasp your shoulder
where the material is torn,
feeling less like a king
than I have for some time.
A little less invincible,
a little less safe.

UNDEFINABLE

We are a fraction, divided by zero,
the movement at the edge of your vision,
your final warning and your last chance.
We are rusted padlocks on chain-link fences,
unkept promises and unread love letters,
the smell of rotting vegetation, tobacco, raw meat.
We are dead celebrities and living politicians,
spit spat onto hot pavements,
the jolt that wakes you and the shadows that linger.
We are railings slick with unknown residue,
stringless guitars strummed tunelessly,
a pane of glass shattered by the body of a bird.
We are the scent of sex in stained sheets,
a three-course meal in a shitty restaurant,
a long-lost sibling with too many memories.
We are a persistent, unidentifiable hum,
a sudden drop in temperature,
a sudden rise in tension.
We are the tip of your tongue, the back of your mind,
just beyond reach and reaching out to you,
and that's just the way we like it.

BURN

This cheap cigarette lighter –
neon pink plastic, chipped and scuffed –
warm from the heat of my hand.
Squeezed tight enough to disappear
through the flesh. Palm imprinted
with red indents, the shape of
space inside a fist. Spark-wheel teeth
shift, shudder, bite into pale thumb skin as I
flick, flick, flick, flame.

This cheap black lipstick – liquid midnight,
three ninety-nine – a gift too late to return.
Bring the fire closer, flush against this
bullet of blank sky. Butane kisses and
burning chemicals. Surface tension shivers,
like a mirage. Molecules tensing away from
the flame. Fat black tears blossoming,
rolling down the casing, clotting in
opaque pools against the sink.

This cheap black heartbreak – a fire –
fast unravelling, the colour of smoke. Bring
the flame closer, as fingertips blister
on the hot metal, as the spark-wheel jams,
as the butane splutters. Each bead of black
is a pearl of sweat, a drop of blood,
a collision-course meteorite
roiling through space. Skin stained like
tarmac at the scene of the crash.

Keep going. Even though the metal
burns, even though the smoke stings,
even though the lipstick stains the porcelain.
Keep going until it is empty. Until all the
liquid is gone. Black fading to grey as
the flame flickers. Then, force your fingers down

your throat and retch bile onto the
white porcelain. Until everything is
empty. Until everything is gone.

CANAL STREET

The neon at the bar is blazing blue;
I never could resist a Friday night.
The old boys in the back are spinning songs,
while I taste cigarette ash on my tongue.
I'm drinking, so I barely feel the cold.
Reality is blurred around its edge.

Outside, I am a blade. I take my edge
and slice the water open, till the blue
comes flowing out to wash away the cold.
The cold so unrelenting, like the night,
the taste of revolution on my tongue.
I've let this city sing her marching songs,

and fill my mind with myths and lies. The songs
that set my long-held principles on edge.
The gin explodes like starlight on my tongue,
behind my eyes the bubbles bursting blue.
There'll be no reassurance from the night.
Sometimes I want to plunge into the cold

and taste the water on my lips. This cold
reminds me of a litany of songs
I've hurled into the bleak November night.
I make my home beside the water's edge
and cradle cans in fingers tinged with blue.
Some say that I have cut away my tongue

or worn it down to silence. No, my tongue
now only moves for those who feel the cold.
A sharpened shifting shard of silver-blue
that ties my mind with misremembered songs.
Invisible, I skim the city's edge
and beg for change while you ignore the night.

I always feel this way on Friday nights,
inertia's blade serrated on my tongue.

Reality is glassy at its edge
like water in the lock, so hard and cold.
I've wrapped myself in all the city's songs,
like bruises on my chest in black and blue.

The cold is creeping round perception's edge,
so drink and sing and gaze beyond the blue
with night still fizzing on my freezing tongue.

A PIECE OF THE PIE

Look,
everyone gets a piece of the pie,
but some get more than others.
It's only fair;
they were here first,
or, if they weren't here first,
then they paid more,
or, if they didn't pay more,
then they certainly looked like
they could afford more,
which is why they got more
at no extra cost.

I wouldn't expect you to understand;
it's complicated.

Some people have asked for more but didn't get it,
while other people could do with less
but won't be persuaded to share.
Some people have been
coming here for years
and think we owe them something.
Some people can't read the menu, so
those people get crumbs.
Some people don't realise
that some people have already eaten.
Some people have already eaten
but still feel the gnawing hunger.
Some people haven't eaten for days.

Everyone gets a piece of the pie,
but some people are never satisfied.
Some people have been stealing food –
someone is always stealing something.
Some slices look bigger than others
because some slices are bigger than others.

Everyone gets a piece of the pie
except those who get nothing,
and we don't mention
those who get nothing
in case they take a piece of our pie.

Sure, some people get more than others,
but some people have more luck than others.
Some people get more pie than others and
some people get crumbs.

It's a good thing it's only pie, isn't it?
It's a good thing it's not our lives, isn't it?
It's a good thing it's not our world, isn't it?
It's a good thing it's only pie.

SEVEN WAYS TO PLEASE YOUR MAN

1.

Film yourself doing something really naughty, like stealing your neighbour's newspaper off their front step, taking stationery from the cupboard at work, or nicking spanners from B&Q. Your man loves it when you don't pay for your tools, you naughty, naughty girl.

2.

Show him you are adventurous. Run out into oncoming traffic; set up an amateur knife-juggling club at your local further education college; disappear for weeks on end without telling anyone where you are. Taunt a rabid dog. Your man won't be able to resist your devil-may-care attitude.

3.

Dress up for him. Try something a bit different, and consider impersonating Franz Ferdinand Carl Ludwig Joseph Maria, the Archduke of Austria and Royal Prince of Hungary and Bohemia, whose assassination in 1914 led to the outbreak of the First World War. After all, men love powerful women, and the false moustache will bring some extra sensory pleasure to the bedroom too.

4.

Talk dirty to him. Tell him that there are over 100 million microbes on your toothbrush, and even more on the underside of your feet. Tell him that over 2.3 billion people across the world don't have access to a flushing toilet, and that, even if they did, over 3 million bacteria per square inch lurk in the average toilet bowl. Tell him that you think he's sexy, despite the fact that his body has 39 trillion bacteria living on it at any one time. Men love receiving compliments!

5.

Use your hands. Have a go at shadow puppetry. Popular shadows include the Duck, the Dog and the Butterfly. But, if you want to get really kinky, why not try the Robust Alligator, the Reluctant Axolotl or the Engorged Badger? Trust me, your man will thank you for it.

6.

Try a new position. Consider becoming a communist, examining capitalism through a paradigm of exploitation, and theorising that class conflict primarily arises from the fundamental imbalance between the proletariat and the bourgeoisie. After all, it pays to be open-minded when it comes to pleasing your man and, when you seize the means of production, he'll give you anything you want.

7.

Try new things. Never repeat yourself. Live up to unrealistic standards of heteronormative sexual gratification, read lists in shitty magazines and follow them as if they were gospel. Try new things. Never repeat yourself.

Or you could just ask him what he likes?

FISH FACE

Of course, we knew that they existed –
in picture books and fairy tales –
but when we finally
dredged one up from the depths
we were more than a little surprised.

She was nothing like we imagined:

no flowing golden hair
and sun-kissed skin.
No silvery voice
or wide submissive eyes.
No pert breasts shielded from sight
behind a seashell bra.

She was nothing like we imagined:

all iridescent scales crusted with
barnacles; wild seaweed-frond hair
and a voice like a hurricane.
Gills and teeth and spines –

more monster than maiden.

She was fascinating, but she would never
make the cover of a magazine.

Still, we lapped up every TV interview,
documentary and podcast, every forward-thinking
thinkpiece and long-form feminist essay.
And, when one Saturday-morning
TV presenter broached the question
of her appearance,
we held our breath…

She said,

My body carries me
across oceans and through storms.
My body can withstand the pressure of
five thousand fathoms of seawater
and swim for six miles without rest.

My body has borne me children
and survived the sharks and
sea monsters of this world.

My body is my instrument.
My body is my weapon.
My body is exactly what I need it to be.

It may not be perfect,
but I am not afraid of it,
because my body is beautiful.

Soon, models were walking the runways
wearing artificial gills, and young people
were saving up to have scales surgically
implanted under their skin.

Green hair dye sold out in shops
and swimming-pool salesmen
struggled to meet the demand.

People prayed for gills and teeth and spines.

The mermaid, realising that humanity had
almost entirely missed the point,
returned to the sea.

CALL AND RESPONSE

I've been staring out to sea again,
perched on the jetty watching the waves,
waiting for my moment.

When the storm-swept chaos subsides –
the sink and swell softens,
roaring winds soothed –
finally, this water will be
tame enough to tread.

Removing my shoes,
I test reality's impermanence,
first with one foot,
then the other,

half convinced this newfound buoyancy
will outperform gravity
if only I choose to let it.

After all, we could all be dead tomorrow,
and it's been so long since I've seen the waves this still.

See, I've been watching the seas
rage and recede for so long,
I almost drowned on dry land.
But now? I think I understand
what I'm supposed to do.

I'm sick of feeling inundated
and floating's not for everyone,
but I will not be submerged again.

I don't care if no one believes me
or if I only stay upright for a moment,
because I am choosing to try,
and that is the opposite of sinking.

STARSTRUCK

Sometimes I get the feeling
maybe we first met in space,
'cause we're both stars,
our constellations shifting into place.
The patterns in this cosmos
match the freckles on your face,
but it's your generosity
that helps me keep my faith.

See, infinity's indelible
and that's intimidating,
but I would wait forever
if you chose to keep me waiting.
We're star-crossed, starstruck, starry-eyed,
you'll get my five-star rating,
but you're not a mass of heat and gas –
that's not what I've been saying!

Instead, I think you're awesome;
you're a blazing supernova
and, like a NASA scientist,
I've tried to get to know you.
Now gravity and love
have got us spinning even closer.
This voyage has been wonderful
and it's still far from over.

I've navigated oceans
on the strength of your advice
(and called you unbelievable
maybe once or twice),
but, though I know astrology's
a little imprecise,
our fate feels universal,
like a starry winter's night.

You're celestial perfection
and to me you're luminous;
if van Gogh was alive,
he'd want to paint the two of us.
So I'm afraid you're stuck with me,
for better or for worse,
and I'll be your observatory
if you'll be my universe.

PSYCHOGEOGRAPHY

Let me tell you a secret:
there is room to think
beyond the space you give yourself.

You are worth more
than you could possibly imagine,
but you have been landlocked for so long
you've almost forgotten what it's like
to trace the water's shadow with your fingertips
and float through life unanchored.

You can still do it. I know you can.

Let's take an adventure in slow motion,
breathe the scent of wood smoke
and let it guide us through the parts of town
no one else sees anymore:

the backs of buildings where
our grandfathers used to work,
the red-brick warehouse once
filled with coal, and the terrace gardens
where our mums hung out washing
like they were hoisting flags.

We'll find crocuses peering
through cracks in the towpaths,
see buses bustling over bridges
and listen as the rush of traffic fades
to a gentle hum, like the sound of the city breathing.

We'll move at a steady pace,
water lapping our edges.
You'll cradle your cup of tea
in freezing fingers and count
the magpies on the banks.

We'll slip through this city,
tasting it on our tongues
and wondering why we don't do this more often.
Wondering why we don't take time
to waste time more often.

We'll unlock this city from the inside,
pass through it almost unnoticed,
leaving nothing but water in our wake,
until it's time to turn ourselves around
and go back home.

SHATTERPROOF

Hope is a patch of sky
reflected through shatterproof glass.

Time sunk into wet concrete,
and countless locks –
clicked closed –
between then and now.

Worlds shrink to the size of a cell.
Days measured in
sun-across-sky shadows
thrown against brick walls;

radio programmes,
visiting hours,
the smell of other men.

Time shifts,
slips through silent hours
like moonlight
through barbed wire

until it's time to start again,
renew, reflect,
embrace the day.

It is so easy to ruminate on emptiness
in these crowded places

where iron bars
creak cold lullabies
and bleach-stink stings
like thoughts of home.

Remember, no matter
how long it takes,
there is still a spark of hope:
a patch of sky reflected
through shatterproof glass.

The scent of fresh air;
a distant open door.

NOTES

Nightclimbing was previously published in Fenland Reed Issue One (2015); In Other Words, Anthology (2016); and in Burning House Press (2016)

Call and Response and *Psychogeography* were both originally commissioned by Nottingham City Council for their 'Enchanted Waters' storytelling project (2019)

Canal Street was previously published in Leftlion Magazine (January 2019)

Shatterproof was previously published by National Justice Museum as part of the 'Desire, love, identity: exploring LGBTQ histories' exhibition (2019)

ACKNOWLEDGEMENTS

Thank you to everyone who has encouraged me and supported me over the last decade of poetry-based adventures. I couldn't have done it without you. And to everyone who feels like they're not good enough: I believe in you. Get out there and do the thing.

Lightning Source UK Ltd.
Milton Keynes UK
UKHW010324170720
366658UK00002B/165